WITH LOVE FOR JACOB

LITTLE DOVES
PEQUEÑAS TÓRTOLAS

SUSAN L. ROTH

The dove calls early in the morning. One long note, and then three short ones. This is his melody, his music, always the same. It's the call of the male. He stands alone on the wire in the pale blue morning, calling to his mate.

El tórtolo canta temprano por la mañana. Una nota larga y luego tres cortas. Esta es su melodía, su música, la cual es siempre igual. Es el canto del macho. Solo, sobre el cable en la mañana azul pálido, él llama a su pareja.

Before you were born, we saw a dove sitting on her unfinished nest of twigs, dried grasses, and wrinkled leaves, on top of the tall pillar near the front door. We watched her through the little round window.

Antes de que nacieras vimos en el alto pilar cerca de la puerta principal, una tórtola sentada sobre su nido a medio terminar, hecho con ramas, hierbas secas, y hojas arrugadas. La observamos por la pequeña ventana circular.

Soon a male dove landed,
crowding her. His beak was
full of the twigs and grasses
and leaves that he was
bringing to his mate. The
female dove used the pieces
to make the nest.

Pronto aterrizó un
tórtolo, rodeándola. Su
pico estaba lleno de las
ramas y hierbas y hojas
que le llevaba a su pareja.
La tórtola usó este
material para construir
el nido.

We looked for the birds every day. Sometimes we would go to the front door and open it silently. The sitting bird would never even blink! We would stare at those big, round, staring eyes and they would stare right back at us.

It's almost impossible to tell the difference between the male and the female. They are both so neat and sleek. They never have a feather out of place.

Estábamos al pendiente de los pájaros todos los días. A veces íbamos a la puerta principal y la abríamos silenciosamente. ¡El pájaro que empollaba ni siquiera parpadeaba! Nosotros mirábamos aquellos ojos grandes, redondos, fijos, y ellos nos devolvían la mirada.

Es casi imposible diferenciar entre el macho y la hembra. Ambos son tan limpios y elegantes. Jamás tienen una pluma fuera de lugar.

These doves only lay two eggs at a time, but they lay them often: up to six sets a season. They make their nests on high places to keep their eggs and themselves safe from cats and people.

Estas tórtolas solo ponen dos huevos a la vez, pero lo hacen a menudo: hasta seis nidadas por estación. Hacen sus nidos sobre lugares altos para proteger sus huevos y cuidarse a ellas mismas de los gatos y la gente.

Male or female, the doves are not good housekeepers. Their nests are very sloppy, but they don't care. They sit still and squarely on their sloppy nests, protecting and warming their little eggs.

Macho o hembra, las tórtolas no cuidan muy bien la limpieza de sus casas. Sus nidos son muy desordenados, pero no les importa. Se sientan quietas y derechas sobre sus desordenados nidos protegiendo y empollando sus pequeños huevos.

The bird on this page
is the actual size of a
real North American
dove (a mourning dove
or Carolina turtle dove,
Zenaida macroura).

El pájaro en esta página
es del tamaño de una
tórtola real de América
del Norte (huilota común
Zenaida macroura).

Day after day,
squinting through
the little round
window, we tried
hard to see their
well-hidden eggs. We
never could. They
had them covered,
completely covered.
All we could see was
the dove, sitting day
and night.

You might think it
never leaves its nest.
But that's not true.
The doves share
their parenting
equally. The male
bird usually sits on
the nest all night.
That gives the female
a chance to eat and
fly and rest.

Día tras día, entrecerrando los ojos, a través de la pequeña ventana circular, tratábamos de ver los huevos tan bien escondidos. Nunca lo logramos. Los tenían cubiertos, completamente cubiertos. Todo lo que podíamos ver era a la tórtola empollando día y noche.

Tal vez pienses que nunca deja su nido, pero no es así. Las tórtolas comparten sus deberes paternales. Usualmente, el tórtolo empolla toda la noche. Así la hembra tiene oportunidad de comer y volar y descansar.

Later, looking through the little round window again, we were almost sure we saw a fuzzy, feathery something moving, brown or grey or both. Somehow it felt as if the little doves were there.

And the day after that, the sweet, tiny things really were there, sitting as still as their parents. The little doves were waiting to be fed.

Más tarde, al volver a mirar por la ventana circular, estábamos casi seguros de ver algo peludo, emplumado, café o gris, moviéndose. De alguna manera se sentía como si las pequeñas tórtolas estuvieran allí.

Al día siguiente, vimos que unas cositas tiernas realmente estaban ahí, sentadas tan quietas como sus padres. Las pequeñas tórtolas esperaban su alimento.

In the beginning little doves eat nothing but the "pigeon milk" that both their parents make and store in their craws. (That's what their throats are called).

But soon the little doves are ready for seeds and grains, the same food that the grownups eat.

Al principio, las pequeñas tórtolas solo comen "leche de paloma" que ambos padres producen y almacenan en sus buches. (Así se llaman sus gargantas).

Pero muy pronto las pequeñas tórtolas están listas para comer las semillas y granos que comen los adultos.

One day we took seeds from the cupboard. We scattered them on the front steps, below the tall pillar.

We ran back inside then, to watch through the little round window. The nest was empty!

Un día tomamos semillas del armario. Las esparcimos sobre los escalones delanteros, debajo del alto pilar.

Luego corrimos hacia adentro para observar por la ventanita circular. ¡El nido estaba vacío!

Back at the front door, we opened it wide to find the little doves on the steps, busy with the seeds.

We frightened them! They flew to a tree, disappearing into the leaves. That was the first time we saw them fly.

Cuando regresamos a la puerta principal, la abrimos de par en par y encontramos a las pequeñas tórtolas en los escalones, ocupadas con las semillas.

¡Las asustamos! Volaron hasta un árbol, desapareciendo entre las hojas. Esa fue la primera vez que las vimos volar.

Inside, we looked out the little round window once again. The little doves were back, too. They were in their nest, staring at us, still as statues.

Ya dentro, miramos por la pequeña ventana circular una vez más. Las pequeñas tórtolas también habían regresado. Estaban en su nido, quietas, como estatuas, mirándonos fijamente.

Late that night, they were still sitting still with their father.

Suddenly it was time for US to fly.

Esa misma noche, ya tarde, ahí estaban todavía quietas, sentadas con su padre.

De repente fue tiempo para NOSOTROS de volar.

And when we ALL came home at last, the birds were home too, watching for you, OUR little dove, in the morning.

Y cuando por fin TODOS regresamos a casa, los pájaros también estaban en su hogar observándote a ti, NUESTRA pequeña tórtola, por la mañana.

Thank you,
D. Adlerman; L. M. Burgess; S. Cresswell; N. Patz; A. L. Roth; P. Senn Yuen.
S.L.R.

Author and Artist: Susan L. Roth, a *New York Times* best-selling author, has written/illustrated more than 55 books for children. Her awards include: the Robert F. Sibert Medal for Nonfiction; *NYT* Best Illustrated Book; Boston Globe-Horn Book Award; Children's Africana Book Award, Africa Access; Arab American Book Award; Green Earth Book Award; and the Jane Addams Children's Book Award.

Translators: Alessandra Narváez Varela is a poet and lecturer in creative writing at the University of Texas at El Paso, and author of the novel *Thirty Talks Weird Love*; and **Héctor Cisneros Vázquez** is a poet from Mexico City, a Fulbright alumnus, and a World Duathlon Championships medalist.

Autora y Ilustradora: Susan L. Roth es una de las artistas y autoras del *New York Times* con más ventas. Ha escrito e ilustrado más de 55 libros. Sus premios incluyen: el Robert F. Sibert Medal for Nonfiction: *NYT* Best Illustrated Book: Boston Globe-Horn Book Award: Children's Africana Book Award, Africana Access: Arab American Book Award: Green Earth Book Award: y el Jane Addams Children's Book Award.

Traductores: Alessandra Narváez Varela es poeta y profesora de escritura creativa en la Universidad de Texas en El Paso, y autora de la novela *Thirty Talks Weird Love;* y **Héctor Cisneros Vázquez** es un poeta de la Ciudad de México, fue becario Fulbright y es medallista del Campeonato Mundial de Duatlón.

Cover collage and CUT OUT font by Susan L Roth. Translation to the Spanish by Alessandra Narváez Varela and Héctor Cisneros Vázquez. Design by Lisa Noudehou. For information, address Barranca Press, USA via editor@barrancapress.com.

April 2021
HC ISBN: 9781939604-361
PB ISBN: 9781939604-163
Library of Congress Control Number: 2021934821
Subject Areas: Dove; Mourning Dove; Birding; New Baby; Birds; Baby Animals; Tórtola; Pájaros; bilingual Spanish and English

Manufactured in the United States of America.

BARRANCA PRESS
Kids' books from here and there

BARRANCA PRESS
Kids' books from here and there

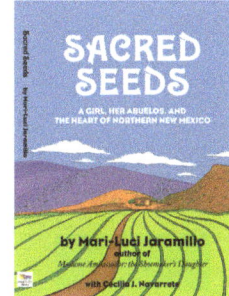

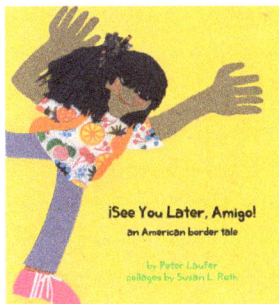

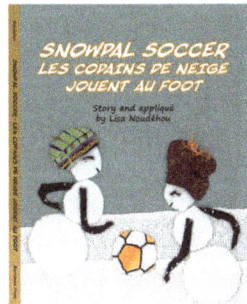

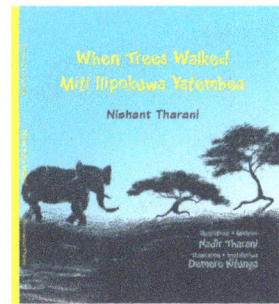

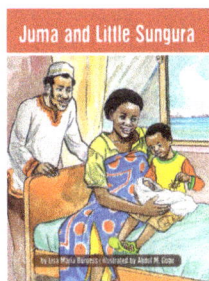

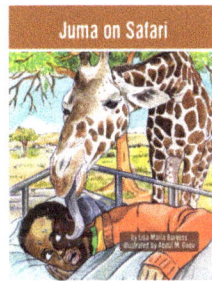

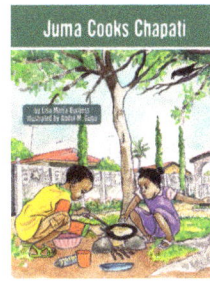

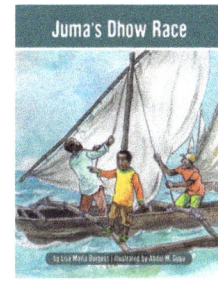

Bilingual English and French:

Playing with Osito | Jouer avec Osito by Lisa Maria Burgess with collages by Susan L. Roth

SnowPal Soccer | Les Copains de Neige Jouent au Foot by Lisa Noudehou

Bilingual English and Spanish:

Playing with Osito | Jugando con Baby Bear by Lisa Maria Burgess with collages by Susan L. Roth

Introducing Spanglish:

¡See You Later, Amigo! an American border tale by Peter Laufer with collages by Susan L. Roth

Bilingual English and Swahili:

When Trees Walked | Miti Ilipokuwa Yatembea by Nishant Tharani with illustrations by Nadir Tharani

Introducing Swahili:

Juma and Little Sungura
Juma on Safari
Juma Cooks Chapati
Juma's Dhow Race by Lisa María Burgess with illustrations by Abdul M. Gugu

English&Spanglish for Middle Grade:

Sacred Seeds: a girl, her abuelos, and the heart of northern New Mexico by Mari-Luci Jaramillo

www.ingramcontent.com/pod-product-compliance
Lightning Source LLC
LaVergne TN
LVHW070841080426
835513LV00024B/2431